This book is a great resource for parents looking to provide their children with healthy recipes while staying on an easy and low budget. Inside you will find some of the best smoothie recipes ever designed specifically for kids, including smoothies that are perfect for breakfast, lunch, dinner and snacks! All of these recipes are simple enough to make at home with minimal effort and ingredients. Best of all, these recipes are packed with nutrients that kids need to stay healthy and energized throughout the day. So, if you're looking for easy and nutritious meals that your children will love, this book is a must-have! You can also rest assured that none of these recipes contain artificial flavours or preservatives. Every smoothie recipe is made with all-natural ingredients and won't cost a fortune to make. With this book, you can provide your children with a healthy and nutritious meal in no time! So, don't wait any longer - get your hands on this book now for the best smoothie recipes ever for kids!

Mango Peach Smoothie

Ingredients:

1 ½ cups almond milk
1 cup diced peaches, fresh or frozen
1 cup chopped mango, fresh or frozen
½ teaspoon vanilla extract
1 cup ice

Mango peach smoothie is a healthy smoothie recipe that kids of all ages will love. Made with nutritious ingredients including almond milk, peaches, mango, vanilla extract, and ice, this smoothie is an excellent way to get your children to consume their daily servings of fruits and dairy without sacrificing flavor. Not only delicious but also very quick and easy to make - simply blend the ingredients together until smooth and enjoy! For added sweetness you can add 1 tablespoon of honey or agave nectar. With its mouth-watering taste, your kids won't even know they are getting so much nutrition in each sip! Enjoy this smoothie as a snack, dessert or an anytime treat.

This smoothie is also vegan and gluten-free, making it a great choice for those on restricted diets. Whether you are looking for smoothie recipes for kids or just something healthy and delicious to enjoy yourself, this mango peach smoothie is sure to be a hit with the whole family! Enjoy!

Blueberry Smoothie

INGREDIENTS:
1 CUP UNSWEETENED VANILLA
ALMOND MILK (OR MILK OF CHOICE)
½ TEASPOON VANILLA EXTRACT
1 CUP FROZEN BLUEBERRIES
1 SCOOP VANILLA PROTEIN
1 LARGE HANDFUL BABY SPINACH
2 TABLESPOONS ALMOND BUTTER
1 TABLESPOON COCONUT FLAKES

If you're looking for a smoothie recipe that is both healthy and kid-friendly, try this Blueberry Smoothie! It's packed with protein, frozen blueberries, almond butter, coconut flakes and baby spinach for an extra nutritional boost. All of these ingredients come together to create a smooth and creamy smoothie that your kids will love. Plus, it only takes 5 minutes to make!

To make the smoothie, combine one cup of unsweetened vanilla almond milk (or milk of choice), ½ teaspoon of vanilla extract, one scoop of vanilla protein powder and two tablespoons of almond butter in a blender. Then add one cup of frozen blueberries and blend until smooth. Finally, stir in one large handful of baby spinach and one tablespoon of coconut flakes. Pour the smoothie into a glass and enjoy!

This smoothie is healthy, delicious, and perfect for kids to enjoy as an afterschool snack or part of a quick breakfast. The combination of plant-based proteins, healthy fats, and antioxidants in this smoothie make it an excellent way to get your kids the nutrition they need while still giving them something tasty! Try this Blueberry Smoothie recipe today to give your family a healthy and enjoyable start to their day.

Coconut Pie Smoothie

INGREDIENTS:

3 BANANAS
¼ CUP ALMOND BUTTER (OR ANY
NUT OR NON-NUT)*
14 OUNCE CAN FULL-FAT
COCONUT MILK
½ CUP COCONUT FLAKES
1 TEASPOON VANILLA EXTRACT
½ CUP ICE

This smoothie recipe for kids is a great way to get them excited about healthy eating! It's packed with creamy coconut milk, bananas, almond butter (or any nut or non-nut of your choice), coconut flakes and vanilla extract. Plus, it can be made in just minutes using only five simple ingredients. Kids will love the tropical flavor of this smoothie that's sure to become a favorite! Just blend together three bananas, ¼ cup almond butter, 14 ounce can full-fat coconut milk, ½ cup coconut flakes and 1 teaspoon vanilla extract with half a cup of ice until smooth. Enjoy this healthy smoothie as an afternoon snack or post-workout treat for kids!

Making smoothies are a great way to get kids involved in the kitchen, and with this smoothie recipe they'll be sure to have a blast. Not only is it healthy and delicious, but also incredibly easy to make – perfect for busy parents looking for quick, nutritious treats! Plus, you can customize it with your favorite nut or non-nut of choice. With its creamy texture and tropical coconut flavor, this smoothie is sure to become a family favorite in no time!

So if you're looking for a smoothie recipe that both adults and kids will love, give this coconut pie smoothie a try. It's packed with good-for-you ingredients like bananas, almond butter (or any nut or non-nut), coconut flakes and coconut milk that will keep everyone energized and satisfied. Plus, it only takes five minutes to make! So what are you waiting for? Let's get blending!

Enjoy!

Pineapple Green Smoothie

1 CUP ALMOND MILK
1 CUP FROZEN PINEAPPLE CHUNKS
2 HANDFULS FRESH SPINACH
1 SCOOP VANILLA PROTEIN

This smoothie is perfect for kids and adults alike! It's a great way to get the benefits of healthy greens while still enjoying a delicious treat. The combination of pineapple, almond milk, spinach, and vanilla protein make this smoothie both healthy and tasty. Plus, it's easy to prepare in just minutes.

To make this smoothie, start by adding one cup of almond milk to your blender. Next, add in one cup of frozen pineapple chunks and two handfuls of fresh spinach. Finally, scoop in one scoop of vanilla protein. Blend all the ingredients together until smooth.

Enjoy your smoothie as a snack or as part of a meal! You can even add a few extras like chia seeds or flaxseeds to make this smoothie even more nutritious. Adding smoothies to your diet is an easy way to get the vitamins and minerals you need while also enjoying something delicious.

Whether you're looking for smoothie recipes for kids or just trying to lead a healthier lifestyle, this pineapple green smoothie is a great option. With just five ingredients and no added sugar, you can have a healthy smoothie in minutes. Enjoy!

Strawberry Cheesecake Smoothie

INGREDIENTS
2 CUPS STRAWBERRIES, SLICED
¾ CUP RAW UNSALTED CASHEWS
1 CUP ALMOND MILK
½ FROZEN BANANA
2 TABLESPOONS LEMON JUICE
1 CUP ICE

This smoothie is perfect for kids - it's healthy and delicious! Preparation of this smoothie couldn't be easier. All you need to do is blend together the strawberries, cashews, almond milk, banana, lemon juice and ice until smooth. Pour your smoothie into a glass and enjoy!

This smoothie recipe is both healthy and delicious, perfect for kids of all ages. Not only that, it's easy to make with only a few simple ingredients! So next time you're looking for a smoothie recipe your kids will love, try out this Strawberry Cheesecake Smoothie. They won't be disappointed!

Enjoy!

Chocolate Peanut Butter Banana Smoothie

INGREDIENTS

1 BANANA, FROZEN
1 CUP MILK OF CHOICE
¼ CUP OLD-FASHIONED ROLLED OATS
3 TABLESPOONS NATURAL PEANUT BUTTER*
1 TABLESPOON COCOA POWDER
CHOCOLATE CHIPS, FOR SERVING (OPTIONAL)

This smoothie recipe is a delicious, healthy treat for kids of all ages. It's easy to make and requires only 5 ingredients: banana, milk of choice, old-fashioned rolled oats, natural peanut butter, and cocoa powder.

To begin preparing the smoothie, take one frozen banana and chop it into small pieces before adding it to a blender. Next, add one cup of your preferred type of milk along with ¼ cup old-fashioned rolled oats, 3 tablespoons natural peanut butter, and 1 tablespoon cocoa powder. Blend until smooth and creamy.

As an optional step, you can also top the smoothie off with some chocolate chips for added sweetness and crunch. Serve immediately and enjoy!

This smoothie is a great way to get your kids to eat something healthy and delicious. For an added nutrient boost, you can also add some flaxseed or chia seeds into the smoothie as well. With five simple ingredients, it's quick and easy to make this smoothie recipe for kids. Enjoy!

Note: If using smooth peanut butter, you may need to add a bit more sweetener. Be sure to read the labels on your ingredients carefully and choose one that is free of added sugars or other unnecessary fillers.

Cinnamon Smoothie

INGREDIENTS

1 CUP UNSWEETENED ALMOND
MILK
1 ½ FROZEN BANANAS, CUT INTO
CHUNKS
¼ TEASPOON CINNAMON, PLUS
MORE FOR DUSTING
½ TEASPOON VANILLA, OPTIONAL
1 TEASPOON BROWN SUGAR,
OPTIONAL
⅓ CUP OLD-FASHIONED OATS
1 CUP ICE

To make it, start by blending the almond milk and frozen banana together until smooth. Then add in the cinnamon, vanilla extract (optional), brown sugar (optional), old-fashioned oats, and peanut butter. Blend until everything is smooth and combined. Finally, add in the cocoa powder and blend for an additional few seconds to combine.

Pour the smoothie into glasses or mugs and top with a sprinkle of cinnamon for garnish. Serve immediately or store any leftovers in the refrigerator for up to 3 days. Enjoy!

This smoothie is a great way to get kids to try new flavors while also giving them a healthy snack. With smoothie recipes like this, you can feel good about offering your kids something nutritious and delicious at the same time. Enjoy!

Bonus Tip: You can make smoothies ahead of time and freeze them in individual containers for easy grab-and-go snacks later!

Peach Smoothie

One of the most delicious smoothie recipes for kids is a peach smoothie. It is healthy, simple to prepare and packed with nutrients. To make this smoothie, you will need 1 ½ cups unsweetened vanilla almond milk, ½ cup Quaker Old Fashioned Oats, 1 teaspoon cinnamon, ¾ cup frozen peaches and 3 ice cubes.

Start by adding the almond milk, oats and cinnamon to a blender. Blend for about 20 seconds until smooth. Then add the frozen peaches and ice cubes and blend again for about 20 seconds until smooth and creamy. Pour into a glass, top with some extra cinnamon or chia seeds if desired, and enjoy! This smoothie recipe can easily be adapted to suit different taste preferences. For a sweeter smoothie, add some honey or agave nectar during blending. To make it more healthy, you can also add in some spinach or avocado for additional nutrients. With this smoothie, kids are sure to get their recommended daily intake of vitamins and minerals!

Enjoy!

!

Strawberry Smoothie

For a strawberry smoothie, you'll need 2 cups of frozen strawberries, 1 banana (room temperature), ¼ cup Greek yogurt*, 1 cup milk (or almond milk or oat milk) and 1 ½ tablespoons of sweetener like maple syrup, honey or agave syrup. Lastly, don't forget to add ½ cup of ice! If your kids like smoothies with a little extra flavor, you can also add 1 tablespoon of almond butter and/or ¼ teaspoon of vanilla. To add a little color and flavor, try adding some fresh mint leaves or basil leaves to the top.

Making smoothies for kids is quick, easy and healthy. Simply blend together all the ingredients until smooth and enjoy! Your kids will love

For smoothie variations, you can try adding different fruits and even vegetables like spinach or kale. If your kids don't like the taste of a certain smoothie, add more of their favorite fruit to make it more palatable. Smoothies are also a great way to sneak in other healthy ingredients like chia, flax or hemp seeds.

Making smoothies for kids is a great way to get them excited about healthy eating and introduce them to new flavors. With just a few simple ingredients, you can create smoothie recipes that are sure to please your little ones! Enjoy!

Chocolate Banana Smoothie

INGREDIENTS

⅓ CUP MILK OF CHOICE (DAIRY OR NON DAIRY)
¼ CUP GREEK YOGURT (FOR VEGAN, OMIT AND
ADD MORE MILK UNTIL IT BLENDS)
2 MEDIUM RIPE BANANAS (ROOM TEMPERATURE)
1 ½ CUPS ICE.
¼ CUP COCOA POWDER.
1 ½ TABLESPOONS MAPLE SYRUP (TO TASTE,
DEPENDING ON THE RIPENESS OF THE BANANAS)
½ TEASPOON VANILLA EXTRACT.

This smoothie is perfect for kids and adults alike! Not only is it healthy, but it's also easy to prepare. To make this smoothie, simply mix all of the ingredients in a blender until smooth. Start by adding the milk, followed by the Greek yogurt if using, and then add the bananas, ice cubes, cocoa powder, maple syrup, and finally the vanilla extract. Blend for several minutes until smooth, adding a bit more milk or yogurt if needed to reach your desired consistency. Once smooth, pour into glasses to serve – it's that easy!

This smoothie is sure to become a favorite in your family. With its yummy combination of chocolate and banana flavors, it's sure to be a hit with the kids. And since it's packed with healthy ingredients like milk, yogurt and bananas, you can feel good about serving it! Enjoy this smoothie as an afternoon snack or even for breakfast – either way, your family is sure to love it!

Watermelon smoothie

This smoothie recipe is perfect for kids and adults alike. It's packed with healthy ingredients like watermelon, strawberries, yogurt, and ice cubes. Plus, it's easy to make in just a few steps.
To prepare this smoothie, first dice the watermelon into 1-inch cubes. Place them into a blender along with the frozen strawberries, ice cubes, and vanilla Greek yogurt. Blend on high until smooth, stopping occasionally to push down the watermelon pieces into the blender if needed.
Once everything is smooth and blended, pour into large glasses and enjoy! This smoothie recipe makes enough for 2-3 servings depending on how much you portion out.
This smoothie is a great way to get kids excited about healthy eating and make smoothie recipes fun. Enjoy!

Good luck!

Pineapple Mango Smoothie

This smoothie is a great way to make a healthy and delicious drink for kids. It's easy to prepare and the ingredients are widely available. To make this smoothie, combine the following ingredients in a blender: water, sugar, mango purée concentrate, pineapple juice concentrate, apple juice concentrate, orange juice concentrate, passion fruit juice concentrate, citric acid, natural flavour, lime juice concentrate and ascorbic acid (vitamin c). Blend until smooth. Serve cold for a refreshing treat.

This smoothie packs all the nutrition and flavor your kids need. It's a great source of antioxidants from the various fruits used to make it. Plus, the smoothie is high in vitamin C from the added ascorbic acid. The smoothie also contains natural sugars from the fruit juice concentrates and a little bit of added sugar for flavor.

This smoothie is easy to make, healthy, and full of delicious flavors that your kids will love! Give it a try today for a nutritious and delicious treat. Enjoy!

Pumpkin Banana Smoothie

INGREDIENTS

1 CUP PUMPKIN PUREE. GREAT
VALUE 100% PURE PUMPKIN, 15 OZ.
1 CUP MILK.
1 BANANA, SLICED.
2 TABLESPOONS BROWN SUGAR.
¼ TEASPOON GROUND CINNAMON.
¼ TEASPOON VANILLA EXTRACT.

This smoothie is a great way to introduce kids to healthy smoothies. It only takes minutes to make and it's full of nutrients that will keep them feeling energized and satisfied.

To prepare the smoothie, combine all ingredients in a blender and blend until smooth. If desired, add a few ice cubes for an extra thick smoothie. You can also top the smoothie with a dollop of whipped cream or sprinkle some cinnamon on top for extra flavor.

This smoothie is full of vitamins, minerals, and antioxidants that make it healthy and delicious. Pumpkin puree provides beta carotene and fiber, banana adds potassium to the smoothie, while the cinnamon and brown sugar add just a touch of sweetness.

This smoothie is sure to be a hit with kids and adults alike! Enjoy it as a healthy snack or even breakfast on the go. You can also freeze leftovers in popsicle molds for an extra special treat.

Happy blending!

Green Smoothie

Green smoothies are a great way to get kids to consume more healthy fruits and vegetables. With just a few simple ingredients, you can make smoothie recipes for kids that are both delicious and nutritious!

To make a kid-friendly smoothie, start by adding 1 1/2 cups of milk or nut milk to your blender. Then add 2 cups of fully packed spinach, 1 banana (frozen is best), 1 apple sliced into pieces, and 1/4 of an avocado. Blend the smoothie until it reaches your desired consistency.

If your kids prefer sweeter smoothies, feel free to add a bit of honey or agave nectar for natural sweetness. For smoothies with even more protein, add a scoop of plant-based protein powder. If they want smoothies that are creamy and filling, try adding nut butter or Greek yogurt.

Once you have the smoothie ready, you can serve it in your favorite smoothie cup or bowl. You can also top it off with fresh fruit slices, nuts, or even a sprinkle of coconut flakes. Kids will love smoothies for breakfast, as an afternoon snack, or even as a healthy dessert!

Making smoothie recipes for kids is fast and easy with just a few simple ingredients. Not only are smoothies delicious and nutritious, but they also make it easier to get your kids to eat more fruits and vegetables. So try making smoothies with your kids today!

Happy blending! :)

Green Pear Smoothie

This smoothie is the perfect recipe for kids who are looking for a healthy and delicious smoothie. It's simple to prepare, full of nutritious ingredients, and tastes amazing. To make it, simply add all the ingredients into a blender: 1 tbsp minced ginger, 1 ripe banana (sliced and frozen), 1 ripe pear (sliced, fresh or frozen), 1/4 cup hemp hearts, 1/4 cup almonds or 2 tbsp almond butter, 2 cups spinach, 1-2 cups of your favorite milk (dairy or plant-based milks work great!), and a pinch of cinnamon. Blend until smooth and enjoy! You can add more milk if desired for a thinner smoothie consistency. With this smoothie recipe, you can be sure your kids are getting a healthy and delicious treat that is packed with nutrients. Enjoy!

Mango And Ginger Smoothie

Mango and ginger smoothies are a healthy, delicious treat that's perfect for kids. Making this smoothie is incredibly easy and requires only a few simple ingredients. Start by gathering the following: 1/2 cup of Quaker® Quick 1-Minute Oats, 1 cup of low fat or fat free milk, 1 cup of fresh or canned mango cubes (peeled, if fresh), 1 can of mandarin orange segments (drained), 2 tablespoons of almond butter, 1 tablespoon of honey, 1 tablespoon of lime juice and 1/2 teaspoon of ground ginger.

To prepare the smoothie, add all the ingredients to a blender or food processor and blend until smooth. Serve the smoothie immediately, or store it in an airtight container for up to 1 day. Enjoy this smoothie as a nutritious breakfast, snack or dessert!

For a fun twist on this smoothie, you can top it with some crunchy granola and fresh fruit. You can also add a few ice cubes to make it a slushy smoothie. With just a few simple ingredients, you can prepare a healthy and delicious smoothie that's sure to please kids of all ages!

Happy smoothie-making! :)

Strawberry Quinoa Smoothie

This smoothie recipe is perfect for kids and health-conscious adults alike. It's packed with superfoods like quinoa, chia seeds, and wheat germ to give your smoothie a nutrient boost. Here's how to prepare it:

First, gather all the necessary ingredients - 1 large ripe banana, 1 (6 oz) low-fat vanilla Greek yogurt, 1/2 cup cooked quinoa (cooled), 2 Tablespoons honey, 1 Tablespoon chia seeds, 1 Tablespoon wheat germ, 2 cups frozen strawberries (if using fresh, freeze them first), and 1-1/2 cups vanilla almond milk.

Next, add the banana, yogurt, honey, chia seeds, wheat germ and almond milk to a blender. Blend until smooth.

Finally, add the quinoa and frozen strawberries to the smoothie and blend again until smooth. Pour into glasses and enjoy!

This delicious smoothie is healthy, tasty and easy to make - perfect for kids or as a healthy snack for adults. Enjoy!

Kale Banana Smoothie

INGREDIENTS:
- 1 ½ CUPS BABY KALE
- 1 SMALL BANANA, SLICED
- 2 TEASPOONS HONEY
- 5 - 6 ICE CUBES
- 1 CUP REDUCED FAT MILK OR NON DAIRY ALTERNATIVE (SUCH AS ALMOND MILK)

This smoothie is an excellent source of calcium, iron and Vitamin A, which are important for healthy growth. It's also a great way to get your kids to enjoy the taste of kale without it being too overpowering. So, whip up a smoothie for breakfast or an after-school snack and watch your kids enjoy this delicious yet healthy treat!

The smoothie is quick and easy to make, so no need to worry about spending too much time in the kitchen. Plus, it's a great way to sneak in some healthy greens into their diet - and they won't even realize it!

Enjoy this smoothie recipe for kids and make sure to experiment with different fruits and vegetables!

Happy blending! :)

Papaya Smoothie

Papaya smoothie is a delicious and healthy smoothie treat that kids will love. It's easy to prepare and only takes a few minutes using simple ingredients like papaya, frozen strawberries, milk, yogurt, honey and ice cubes. Here is how to make this smoothie:

1. Gather all of your ingredients - 1/2 of a medium papaya, peeled, seeded and chopped (3/4 cup), 1/2 cup Cascadian Farm™ organic frozen strawberries, 1/2 cup fat-free milk, 1/2 cup Yoplait® fat-free plain yogurt, 1 tablespoon honey and 3 large ice cubes.

2. Place the papaya, frozen strawberries and milk into a blender. Blend until smooth.

3. Add in the yogurt, honey and ice cubes to the smoothie mix. Pulse blend until smooth.

4. Serve chilled in a tall glass with some papaya or strawberry slices (optional) and fresh mint leaves on top (optional). Enjoy your smoothie!

By making your smoothie with healthy ingredients, you can make sure that your kids are getting the nutrition they need while treating them to a delicious smoothie. Papaya smoothies are an easy and healthy smoothie recipe for kids that can be made in minutes. Enjoy!

Blackberry Yogurt Smoothie

This smoothie is a healthy and delicious treat the whole family will enjoy. It's easy to make, so it's perfect for busy days when you need something nutritious on-the-go. With blueberries, blackberries, banana, soy milk and Greek yogurt as its key ingredients, this smoothie provides essential vitamins and minerals that are important for healthy growth and development. It's a great smoothie recipe for kids to help them get the nutrients they need.

To prepare the smoothie, simply add all of the ingredients into a blender or food processor and blend until smooth. Serve immediately in glasses or pour it into portable containers to take with you on-the-go. Enjoy this smoothie as a healthy snack or meal replacement.

Green Grape Smoothie

Making smoothies is an easy and healthy way to get kids excited about eating fruits and vegetables. This green grape smoothie recipe is a great choice for kids because it's packed with nutritious ingredients that also taste delicious.

To make this smoothie, first freeze the green grapes ahead of time if you prefer a colder smoothie. Then, add 1/2 cup of fresh baby spinach to the measuring cup. Next, add 1/2 cup Greek yogurt and 1/2 cup Noble 100% Florida Tangerine Juice. Finally, add 1 cup of ice and 2 tablespoons honey to taste.

Blend all ingredients together until smooth. Divide evenly into two glasses and enjoy your smoothie!

This smoothie is a great way to introduce kids to healthy ingredients. Not only does it contain green grapes, spinach, Greek yogurt and tangerine juice, but by adding honey, the smoothie also has a hint of sweetness that will appeal to picky eaters. Plus, it's easy to prepare and takes only minutes to make.

So, if you're looking for smoothie recipes for kids that are healthy and delicious, try this green grape smoothie and watch your little ones enjoy it!

Happy smoothie-making!

Kiwi Apple Smoothie

INGREDIENTS

1 SMALL APPLE, PEELED, CUT INTO CHUNKS.
1 KIWIFRUIT, PEELED, CUT INTO CHUNKS.
4 MEDIUM FRESH STRAWBERRIES.
2/3 CUP YOPLAIT® 99% FAT FREE CREAMY
STRAWBERRY YOGURT (FROM 2-LB CONTAINER)
1/3 CUP APPLE JUICE.

Kiwi apple smoothie is a great smoothie option for kids. This recipe uses ingredients that are healthy and easy to obtain, making it perfect for busy families. To make the smoothie, start by peeling and cutting an apple into chunks. Place the apple pieces in a blender, followed by one kiwifruit peeled and cut into chunks. Add four medium fresh strawberries, two-thirds cup Yoplait® 99% Fat Free creamy strawberry yogurt from a two-pound container, and one-third cup apple juice. Blend all the ingredients until smooth. Serve immediately for a tasty smoothie with added fruit and protein! Kids will love this smoothie recipe that is both healthy and delicious!

Adding smoothies like the Kiwi Apple smoothie to your family's diet is a great way to ensure that everyone gets the essential vitamins, minerals and nutrients they need. You can also adjust this recipe by adding different flavors of yogurt or juice, depending on your family's tastes. So why not try out this smoothie recipe today? It's sure to be a hit with the whole family!

For smoothie recipes for kids that are both healthy and delicious, look no further than a kiwi apple smoothie. With just a few ingredients and easy instructions, you can create this smoothie quickly and easily. And your kids will love it too!

Strawberry Peach Smoothie

This smoothie is a great way to start your day! Not only is it healthy, but it's also easy to put together and can be a great smoothie recipe for kids. To make this smoothie, you will need: 1/2 cup ice cubes, 1/2 cup frozen strawberries, 1/2 cup frozen peaches, 1/4 cup fresh sliced banana, 1/4 cup plain, unsweetened Greek yogurt, and 3/4 cup orange juice.

Start by adding the ice cubes to a blender. Then add in the frozen strawberries and peaches. Next, add in the banana slices. Finally pour in the Greek yogurt and orange juice. Blend all the ingredients together until smooth. Serve immediately and enjoy this smoothie throughout your day!

This smoothie is a great option for everyone, especially those on the go! It has just the right amount of sweetness and can provide you with enough energy to power through your day. You can adjust the smoothie's flavor by adding more or less fruit and juice depending on your taste preferences. Enjoy!

Avocado Smoothie

Avocado smoothie is a healthy and delicious smoothie recipe that can be enjoyed by kids and adults alike. To prepare this smoothie, you will need 1/2 of a large avocado, 1 1/2 cups cold milk of choice, scant 1 tsp pure vanilla extract, sweetener of choice such as 2 tbsp pure maple syrup or stevia to taste, 1/8 tsp salt and a scoop of protein powder (optional).

Start by adding the avocado and milk into a blender or food processor. Blend until smooth, then add in the vanilla extract, sweetener of choice, salt and optional protein powder. Blend everything together until smooth. Serve chilled for best results! Avocado smoothie is a great snack or breakfast option for both kids and adults. Enjoy!

Banana And Almond Butter Smoothie

Banana and almond smoothie is a quick, healthy and delicious smoothie recipe for kids. It's packed with nutrition from the banana, almond milk and almond butter and can be made in minutes.

To make this smoothie, you will need 1 small frozen banana, 1 cup unsweetened almond milk, 2 tablespoons of almond butter, 2 tablespoons unflavored protein powder, 1 tablespoon of sweetener (optional), 1/2 teaspoon ground cinnamon and 4-6 ice cubes.

First, blend the banana and almond milk in a blender until smooth. Then, add the almond butter, protein powder and sweetener (if using). Blend again until smooth. Finally, add the cinnamon and ice cubes to the smoothie mixture and blend until smooth.

Your smoothie is now ready to enjoy! This smoothie is a great way to get your kids their daily dose of fruits, fiber, protein, vitamins and minerals. Enjoy this delicious smoothie as an afternoon snack or post-workout beverage. Bon Appetit!

Peanut Butter Chocolate Smoothie

INGREDIENTS

1/4 CUP LOW FAT MILK (OR ALMOND OR NON DAIRY MILK)
1 BANANA, SLICED AND FROZEN (ABOUT 1 CUP SLICES)
1 TABLESPOON LIGHT CREAMY PEANUT BUTTER.
1 TABLESPOON COCOA POWDER.
HONEY, OPTIONAL AND TO TASTE IF DESIRED.

This smoothie is a great way to make sure your kids get a healthy start to their day! The creamy peanut butter and cocoa powder give it a delicious flavor, while the banana and milk add some fiber and protein. Plus, it's easy to prepare - just blend all of the ingredients together until smooth! And if you want to make it sweeter, add a bit of honey to taste. Enjoy!

This smoothie is perfect for breakfast, snack time, or any time you need a healthy and delicious treat. Kids love it because of the sweet chocolatey flavor, and parents will love that it's packed with nutrients. So next time you're looking for smoothie recipes for kids, give this peanut butter chocolate smoothie a try! Your little ones will thank you. Enjoy!

Banana Berry Smoothie

This Homemade Banana-berry Smoothie is a smoothie recipe that kids will love! It's simple to make and full of healthy, natural ingredients. Plus, it's packed with vitamins, minerals, antioxidants and protein. To prepare this smoothie, start by gathering the ingredients: 1 medium or large ripe banana, ½ cup frozen blueberries, 4 fresh or frozen strawberries, hulled, 1 cup milk, 1 teaspoon honey and 2-3 ice cubes if desired. Peel the banana and cut it into slices. Put all the ingredients in a blender and blend until smooth. Pour into glasses and enjoy! This smoothie is packed with healthy fruits and nutrients that your kids will love! Plus, it's an easy way to get them to eat more fruits and vegetables. If you want to add a bit of sweetness, you can drizzle some honey on top for a delicious treat. Enjoy!

Spinach And Pear Smoothie

This spinach and pear smoothie is a healthy smoothie recipe that will have kids wanting more! It's easy to make and packed with nutrients. To prepare this smoothie, blend 1 cup milk of choice, ½ cup plain Greek yogurt, 2 cups spinach, 1 medium ripe pear core removed (skin on), 1 ripe banana, ¼ teaspoon ground cinnamon and 1 cup ice until smooth. For added nutrition, you can also add in chia seeds, hemp seeds, flax seeds, protein powder, honey or peanut butter to customize this smoothie according to your family's preferences. Enjoy!

This smoothie is a great way to sneak veggies into your kids' diets while making a healthy and delicious snack. Enjoy it for breakfast, as an afternoon pick-me-up or as a post-workout smoothie to refuel your body. Satisfying and nutritious, this smoothie is sure to become a favorite of both young and old! For even more smoothie recipes that kids will love, check out our other smoothie recipes. You can easily make smoothies with your favorite fruits and veggies for a healthy and delicious treat any time of day!

Happy smoothie-making! :)

Orange Smoothie

Ingredients
4 fresh oranges, peeled.
2 cups ice.
1/3 cup milk (your preference - regular, soy,
coconut, etc.)
1-2 tablespoons honey (or agave or your
desired sweetener), if needed.
1 teaspoon vanilla extract, store-bought or
homemade.

Making smoothies at home is a great way to keep kids healthy, and an orange smoothie is especially refreshing. This smoothie recipe for kids takes only minutes to make and is not only delicious - it's also packed with vitamins, minerals and antioxidants.

To make this smoothie recipe for kids, start by peeling four fresh oranges and chopping them into chunks. Put the orange pieces in your blender, then add two cups of ice, 1/3 cup of milk (you can use regular cow's milk, soy milk or coconut milk), 1-2 tablespoons of honey (or agave syrup if needed for extra sweetness) and a teaspoon of vanilla extract. Blend until smooth and creamy.

If your smoothie is too thick, add a bit more milk until you get the desired consistency. Serve immediately for a delicious, healthy smoothie that your kids will love! Enjoy!

Coconut And Berry Smoothie

Coconut and Berry smoothie is a delicious and healthy smoothie recipe that's perfect for kids. It's simple to make and bursting with flavor! To prepare this smoothie, simply combine all the ingredients in a blender: one heaping cup of frozen mixed berries (blackberries, raspberries, strawberries, blueberries), 2/3 cup of light coconut milk or almond milk, 1/2 banana (fresh or frozen), 1 tablespoon of soaked chia seeds (1 teaspoon dry), 1 tablespoon of fresh orange or tangerine juice, and 1 teaspoon of fresh lime juice. Blend until smooth and enjoy! This smoothie is an excellent way to start off the day with plenty of healthy vitamins and minerals. It's also a great after-school snack that will provide energy and nourishment for kids on the go! Try it today and see how delicious healthy smoothies can be!

Beet And Berry Smoothie

Ingredients
½cup freshly squeezed orange juice.
1cup mixed frozen berries or blueberries.
2tablespoons granola.
⅓cup diced beet, either raw or roasted (50 grams)
¼cup plain low-fat yogurt or low-fat coconut milk.
1teaspoon honey or agave syrup.
2 or 3ice cubes.
sliced orange for garnish (optional)

Smoothies are a great way to introduce kids to healthy eating habits. This beet and berry smoothie is a delicious, nutritious treat for the whole family! It's made with wholesome ingredients like freshly squeezed orange juice, mixed frozen berries or blueberries, granola, diced beet (raw or roasted), plain low-fat yogurt or low-fat coconut milk, honey or agave syrup and ice cubes. To make it fun for the kids, top off with a few slices of orange for garnish.

To prepare this smoothie recipe for kids, simply blend all the smoothie ingredients together in a blender until smooth. Pour into glasses and serve cold with the optional orange slices for garnish. Enjoy this healthy smoothie as an afternoon snack or even a breakfast smoothie - it's sure to be a hit with the whole family!

This smoothie is packed full of nutrients that are essential for maintaining good health and promoting healthy growth in kids. The oranges provide vitamin C and fiber, while the berries offer up antioxidants. The yogurt or coconut milk adds protein and healthy fats, while the beet gives an extra boost of vitamins and minerals. All in all, it's a delicious smoothie that's sure to keep your kids feeling energized throughout the day!

Chocolate And Peanut Butter Smoothie

Chocolate and peanut butter smoothie recipes for kids are one of the most delicious and healthy treats you can make. Preparing this smoothie is fast and easy, with minimal ingredients. To start, gather 1/4 cup low fat milk (or almond or non dairy milk), 1 banana that has been sliced and frozen (about 1 cup slices), 1 tablespoon light creamy peanut butter, 1 tablespoon cocoa powder, and honey (optional and to taste if desired).

In a blender or smoothie machine, blend the milk and frozen banana slices until smooth. Add in the peanut butter and cocoa powder, blending until combined. Taste the smoothie for sweetness and adjust with honey as desired. Your smoothie is now ready to enjoy!

For an extra special treat, try adding in some fresh berries or a sprinkle of mini chocolate chips. Chocolate and peanut butter smoothies are sure to be a hit with kids and adults alike! Plus, they provide the perfect healthy snack for any time of day. Enjoy!

Thank you

We hope you enjoyed
our book.

As a small family company ,your
feedback is very important to us.

Please let us know how you like
your book

www.ingramcontent.com/pod-product-compliance
Lightning Source LLC
LaVergne TN
LVHW070955180726
843512LV00017B/1247